# SCANDINAVIA
## A PICTURE MEMORY

**Text**
Bill Harris

**Photography**
Colour Library Books Ltd.
Stenders Forlag, Denmark
Aune Foto-Arkiv, Norway

**Captions**
Laura Potts

**Editorial**
David Gibbon

**Design**
Teddy Hartshorn

**Director of Production**
Gerald Hughes

CLB 3267
© 1993 CLB Publishing, Godalming, Surrey, England.
All rights reserved.
This 1993 edition published by Magna Books,
Magna Road, Wigston, Leicester, England.
Colour separations by Scantrans Pte Ltd, Singapore
Printed and bound by Leefung Asco, Hong Kong
ISBN 1-85422-494-8

# SCANDINAVIA

## A PICTURE MEMORY

MAGNA
BOOKS

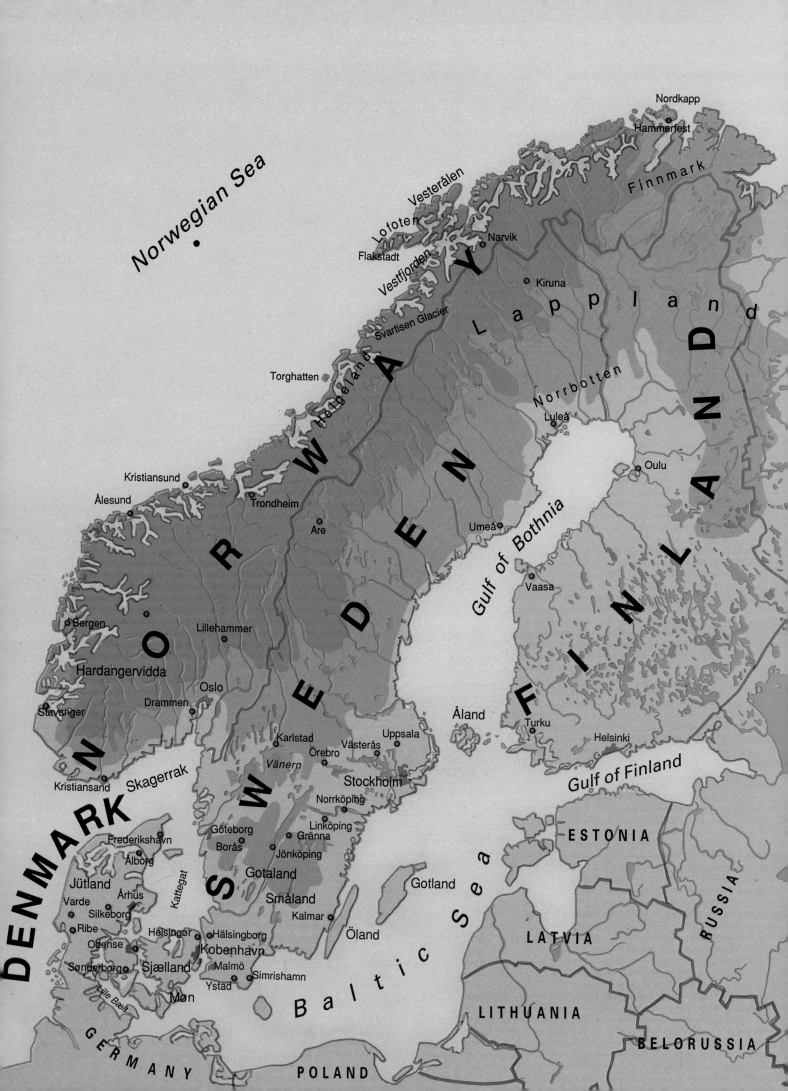

The year AD 793 was not a good one in the north of England. According to a contemporary record, there were mysterious whirlwinds, the night sky was filled with strange phantom lights, the land was scorched by the fiery breath of dragons and famine stalked the countryside. And that was all in just the first five months. "On 8 June of the same year," says the chronicle, "merciless heathens laid waste the Church of God in Lindisfarne, with plundering and killing."

The merciless heathens were farmers from the coast of Denmark out looking for some fun and adventure. It had become customary for the men of Sweden, Norway and Denmark to "go Viking" in their long boats as soon as their crops were in, and not go home again until it was time for harvesting. The raid at Lindisfarne was the first one anyone had noticed … or, more accurately, lived to write about. The longships from the north made regular summer trips to plunder the British Isles after that, and in a few years they began appearing on the coast of France, with the same results. And everywhere they went they were despised as heathens and feared as barbarians. It was true that some of their ancestors had been the most warlike of the Germanic tribes, the Goths, the Teutons and the Vandals, who overran the Roman Empire, a classical example of barbarism. And it was also true that they were heathens, but only in the religious sense because they had been neglected by Christian missionaries and not because they were uncivilized. There is evidence that humans were domesticating animals, clearing forests for towns and planting crops in Sweden and Denmark as far back as 3000 BC, and that they were trading with the early Mediterranean civilizations a thousand years later.

The Greek explorer, Pytheas, landed on the coast of Norway in 350 BC and described the land he called "ultima Thule," the end of the world, as a place of frozen seas, a never-setting summer sun and months of darkness in winter. Of course, nobody believed him. They were also skeptical when he said that the people there made a quite pleasing drink from honey and barley, and that they built huge buildings so they could thresh their grain indoors. His friend Strabo, the famous Greek geographer, said that Pytheas was only spinning fairy tales and that his stories shouldn't be taken seriously. But the Romans, who found it difficult to take any culture seriously except their own but were fascinated by the things they could take from other cultures, found a rare treasure in Scandinavia. The coasts of the Baltic and the North Sea were rich in amber – fossilized tree resin – and, although the early Scandinavians had been carrying the translucent material overland to Mediterranean jewelers for centuries, the Romans streamlined the trade by sending ships up the European coast for more of it. They also found rare furs in the far north, and because they were prized by Roman patricians, they exchanged gold and silver as well as jewels and other treasures from their empire for them. They weren't above capturing a few slaves here and there, but the relationship between Rome and "ultima Thule" was mostly a business proposition, because the Celts and Germans controlled the territory that separated them. It was a perfectly normal state of affairs for the Scandinavians. Their remote location and their climate had made them relatively safe from foreign invaders for centuries, and if their cousins to the south added to their isolation, they didn't mind a bit.

It was because of their isolated existence that the rest of Europe was so surprised to hear from the Scandinavians in the ninth century. Until a few hundred years earlier they had been scratching out a meager existence for themselves up there at the end of the world, and when they went to war it was usually with one another. When the Romans penetrated their land they found iron in the bogs of Norway and taught the Scandinavians how to use it. Tools made from the new metal made farming easier and completely changed their way of life. More efficient farming not only raised the standard of living, but it also encouraged people to move out of their tight communities and spread across the land. Even so, Scandinavia wasn't the richest farm land in the world, and the search for better soil eventually gave the Scandinavians their wanderlust. And it was their new-found skill with iron, along with the power vacuum created by the fall of the Roman Empire, that made it possible for them to satisfy the urge. Iron axes made it possible for them to carve solid oak beams into sea-worthy vessels that could take them just about anywhere in the world they wanted to go. Their earliest voyages out of Norway and Denmark, like the one that took them to the north of England, were for pure adventure, but before long the Viking raiders began to realize that they didn't have to head for home at harvest time. And when it dawned on them that they could produce better harvests in these new lands where the climate in winter was milder, they became colonizers instead of pirate raiders.

The first great wave of them went east from Sweden and began building colonies in Finland as bases for pushing further inland. These Vikings, who called themselves "Men of Rus," characterized themselves as protectors of the Slavic people who were already there, and once their new capital at Kiev was built they never looked back across the Baltic. Instead they looked east, and when they saw the great cities of the Byzantine Empire, they knew what they had to do. Their attacks were savage, but the Byzantine emperor was a skilled politician who negotiated a treaty with the Vikings that allowed them free access for trade, but limited it to a few months a year and forced a promise from the Men of Rus that they'd only come in small groups. In time, a Slavic queen would charm the Byzantines into a friendlier treaty and introduce Orthodox Christianity into her land, which was by then called Russia. But the whole process began with Viking raiders who pushed their own influence beyond Constantinople and into the Middle East.

The Norwegians and Danes, meanwhile, headed west. Within less than fifty years they were the masters of most of the British Isles and were putting down roots at the edge of mainland Europe, in the northwestern corner of France. This territory was given by the French kings to the Vikings in 911, in hope they wouldn't take more. At the same time, their amazing boats took them across the Atlantic to Greenland, Iceland and the tip of North America itself.

Most of the wanderers were basically interested in finding land more hospitable to their iron plows, but their iron axes made them formidable warriors, too, and the people they encountered in their travels were generally terrified of them. But if their methods may have seemed uncivilized, the truth about the people themselves was

quite the opposite. They had a genius for colonizing, an interesting talent considering that no other culture had ever colonized their own homeland, and their organizational skills made their colonies flourish. They established profitable trading posts on the coasts of Ireland and Wales, created productive farms in England and Scotland, and their towns in Normandy made the French king sorry he had given them the opportunity to settle at the edge of his country.

But the greatest achievement of the Viking Age, at least for the folks back home, came in 874, when a Norwegian ship was blown off course and washed ashore on the coast of Iceland. Within a half century, more than 20,000 Scandinavians were living in the biggest of all the Viking colonies. Ironically, before the Vikings arrived, a handful of intrepid Irish monks had already sailed to Iceland in search of the peace and quiet they believed the Norse invaders had taken from them, and now here they were again. But this was a peaceful invasion, and although the Viking chieftains ruled with iron hands, they established a code of laws with a central parliament and a system of courts, an unusually enlightened idea at the time. But it was based on an idea that had been a way of life in Scandinavia for generations. Although the land was divided into feudal estates, democracy had come early and the people were never completely without a voice in their own affairs.

One idea that did arrive late in Scandinavia, however, was Christianity. The colonizing Vikings frequently converted to the religion of the lands they settled in, but it wasn't until the end of the tenth century that the kings of Norway, Sweden and Denmark decided to do the same, and their subjects, frequently by force, followed them in denouncing the old gods. But one message of Christianity that the kings missed was that they should love their neighbors. After the Norwegians exiled their king, Erik Bloodax, in the 940s, the Danish king, Harald Bloodtooth, defeated his successor and turned the throne over to Greyfur, one of Bloodax's sons. In spite of Greyfur's obligation to Denmark, he kept Norway independent during his reign as King Harald II. The Danes were always lurking in the background, however, and finally, in the year 1000, the Danish monarch joined forces with the king of Sweden, Olav the Taxgatherer, and together they defeated the Norwegians, dividing the captured kingdom between them.

In the meantime, governments in other parts of the world had become stronger and more centralized, and it wasn't as easy for small bands of adventurers to grab riches and power wherever their boats happened to touch shore, so the Scandinavian raiders began heading for home. The age of the Vikings was over.

Among the repatriates was Olav Haraldsson, a descendant of Harald Fairhair, the first of the Norwegian kings. Appalled to find his country controlled by outsiders, he organized the farmers of the east to create a new kingdom, but more opposed him than supported him and he was killed by his own peasant army. It wasn't long, though, before the Norwegians had a change of heart. King Canute, the Danish king, had sent his teenage son to rule them, and added insult to injury by sending an English woman to keep an eye on the boy and his subjects. Suddenly, the dead Olav began to look like a hero. Exactly a year after he was killed his body was removed to the high altar of the church at Nidaros, now Trondheim, and he was declared a saint. Although never formally canonized, and never the king of all Norway, he is the patron saint of the country and a symbol of its united kingdom. But if the Norwegians had objected to being ruled by a teenager, none of them gave a second thought to proclaiming Olav's son, Magnus, their new king. But then, Magnus wasn't a teenager. He was eleven years old. It didn't seem strange to them, either, that their new king made a pact with the Danish monarch to the effect that, on the death of either of them, the survivor would rule both countries. Naturally, Magnus outlived his Danish counterpart, and when he took over the dual throne in 1042 he also became king of England. His uncle, Harald III Hardraade, inherited his power and kept England under his Scandinavian thumb until his cousins, the Normans, moved across the Channel in 1066.

Over the next several centuries it was the Germans who exerted the lion's share of influence over the countries to the north through its powerful merchants on the Baltic coast. Things began changing for the better in 1397, when Margrethe, the daughter of the Danish king, married the Norwegian king and became monarch of both countries, quickly annexing Sweden, too, and creating what became known as "the Union of the Three Crowns," that would last for more than a hundred years.

The tales of the Norse kings are known as sagas, which is an old Scandinavian word meaning to move slowly. But over the centuries, the comings and goings of the rulers of Sweden, Norway and Denmark are a series of fast-changing events, of bloody intrigues and chicanery, of child regents and shifting power that sometimes brought the three countries together and sometimes put them at each other's throats. And the saga continued right through to the end of the 18th century.

By the beginning of the century Norway had almost ceased to exist after more than three hundred years of Danish rule. When Denmark sided with the French in the Napoleonic Wars, the Norwegians were dragged into it, but their neighbors, the Swedes, fought on the other side. When the wars ended and Sweden was forced to give up her Finnish colonies to the Russians, the loss was counterbalanced by an offer to take Norway instead. Of course, the Norwegians weren't at all pleased, and in 1814 they drafted their own constitution, giving themselves the right to elect their own king. The Swedes considered it a revolutionary act and sent in their army, but after a short war they agreed to let the constitution stand if the newly elected king – a Dane, by the way – would agree to abdicate. For the next ninety years the Norwegians who had been ruled from Copenhagen for so long, served new masters based in Stockholm. The saga came to an end in 1905 with a Norwegian declaration of independence. Neither country was in the mood for war, and the divorce was accomplished with the stroke of a pen. It was followed by an election that made Prince Carl of Denmark their king, and as Haakon VII he established the first Norwegian royal line for six hundred years. It also formalized the division of the three Scandinavian countries of Denmark, Sweden and Norway as they exist today.

During World War I all three countries stayed neutral, and Scandinavia was spared the devastation that ruined most of the rest of Europe. But in the 1930s their neutrality was compromised when Hitler's armies invaded both Denmark and Norway. The Danes were forced to surrender in the face of a threat to level Copenhagen, and although the Norwegians fought on, they, too, were brought down when Allied help was diverted after the fall of France. Sweden, meanwhile, held on to her neutrality by allowing the Nazis to use her territory and to buy raw materials. King Haakon of Norway set up a government-in-exile in London, and directed a fierce anti-Nazi underground movement from there; and King Christian X of Denmark led his people on a course of passive resistance that eventually grew into a highly effective clandestine war machine.

When the war ended, Scandinavia was as devastated as the rest of Europe, but it was also the first to recover. By the mid-1950s Norway's industrial output was more than double what it had been when Hitler moved in. In Denmark, which had fewer natural resources but the same brand of determination, the gain was about thirty percent, and Sweden was well on its way to becoming one of the most productive industrial nations in the world. In 1952, the Scandinavian countries, already closely linked by similar languages and the common religion of Lutheranism, joined together to form the Nordic Council to formalize cooperation between their governments. It combined all of Scandinavia into a common labor pool and provided for collaboration in dealing with such things as protecting the environment and providing electricity and highway links without regard for national boundaries. But if the Scandinavian countries were once again influencing outsiders with their unity and their industries, they never lost their love for nature and the great outdoors.

Although the majority of modern Nordic people live in cities, more of them own weekend homes than any other Europeans, and they never seem happier than when they are out enjoying the countryside. It is a countryside filled with Europe's biggest forests and its greatest concentration of lakes. It is a land surrounded by thousands of miles of rugged seacoast, punctuated by hundreds of thousands of forest-covered offshore islands. By custom, all of the open land – and there are millions of square miles of it – is accessible to everyone with an urge to smell some wildflowers, to pick some berries or mushrooms, or just to lie in the grass and watch the clouds roll by.

Many also enjoy the thrill of searching the woodlands for gnomes. In other places, such hunts are considered frivolous, but in Scandinavia, where nothing is ever frivolous, it is a serious business. The object of the search is a race of little men with snowy white beards, and pointed red hats that double their six-inch height. Their faces are wrinkled with what some say are laugh lines, although few humans have ever heard one laugh. Almost no one has ever seen a female gnome, either, but they obviously exist, because although a gnome's life expectancy is only four hundred years, the race has existed in Scandinavia for thousands. They live close to nature in tiny houses filled with all sorts of labor-saving devices they invented themselves. They make fine furniture without nails, produce high-quality glassware and beautiful ceramics. They are master metal-workers and building machines is second nature to them. They can run faster and jump higher than any human, and their strength is equal to seven men. And although they are naturally competitive, no gnome is considered superior to another, and because of their social structure none is either richer or poorer than another.

It all adds up to an almost perfect description of the average Scandinavian, whose lifestyle is almost too good to be true.

*The famous nineteenth-century Danish storyteller, Hans Christian Andersen, is commemorated by the statue, The Little Mermaid (facing page), in Denmark's capital, Copenhagen. Edvard Eriksen's lovely bronze figure, located at Langelinie, has become one of the symbols of the city.*

A statue (above) in the Danish capital Copenhagen pays tribute to Bishop Absalon, the twelfth-century bishop regarded as one of the city's founding fathers. Christiansborg Palace (above right and facing page bottom), seat of the Danish Parliament and the Supreme Court, stands on the same site as Absalon's original fortress. The city offers many architectural gems, including the Town Hall (right), the Exchange (below right), Rosenborg Palace (below), and Amalienborg Palace (facing page top). Overleaf: an aerial view of Copenhagen.

Copenhagen (these pages) is one of Scandinavia's most charming cities. Fine religious architecture such as the Marble Church (above) combines with historic buildings like the Round Tower (left) and picturesque districts such as Christianshavn (above left) to give the city its unique character. Among Copenhagen's attractions are the superb State Museum of Art (below left) and the world-famous Tivoli Gardens (below). Facing page top: Nyhavn, lined with gabled houses. Facing page bottom: the Anchor Memorial, at the upper end of Nyhavn.

15

*Møns Klint (below), on the eastern coast of the island of Møn, is one of Denmark's most popular tourist attractions. The spectacular chalk cliffs, which reach 420 feet at their highest point, stand out in stark contrast to the deep blue of the sea. Denmark's great natural beauty is complemented by her rich historical heritage. Fredensborg Palace (center right), Frederiksborg Castle (right) and Kronborg Castle (below right) at Helsingør are just a few of the historic buildings in the region of Zealand.*

A statue of the writer Hans Christian Andersen (above) stands proudly in Odense, the principal town on the Danish island of Funen. Andersen was born in Odense, and his birthplace (above left), a small house on Hans Jensens Stræde, is now a museum. The nearby fishing town of Kerteminde (facing page bottom) acted as Odense's port until the beginning of the nineteenth century. Svendborg (below, below left and facing page top), in Funen, displays the half-timbered buildings that characterize the island. Left: the bridge across Lillebælt.

Historic towns on the peninsula of Jutland are evidence of Denmark's rich and varied past. Frederikshavn (above) and Viborg (right) boast lovely churches, while both Ribe (below) and Århus (above right) have magnificent twelfth-century cathedrals. In the town of Ålborg, buildings like Jens Bang's Stone House (below right), a Renaissance masterpiece, have been preserved. Facing page top: the windswept coast at Varde. Facing page bottom: the town of Silkeborg, in central Jutland.

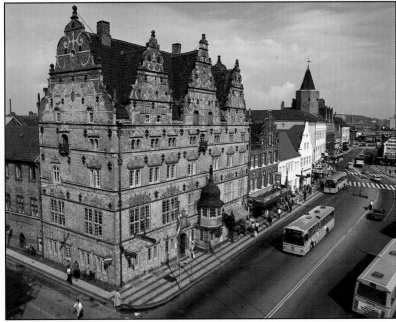

Skåne (these pages), Sweden's most southerly region, remained part of Denmark until 1658, and Danish influences are reflected in much of its architecture, notably Glimmingehus Castle (left). Charles X, the king whose victory against the Danes ensured the generous terms of the Treaty of Roskilde, winning for Sweden the fertile lands of Skåne, is commemorated by an imposing statue in Malmö's main market square (below). Facing page: picturesque streets in the historic town of Ystad. Overleaf: fields of unripe wheat in Skåne, the "granary of Sweden."

From Brahe Hus Castle (below) there is a fine, panoramic view of the rich farmland for which southern Sweden is noted. Skåne, the region at the southernmost tip of Sweden, boasts some charming towns, among them the ancient port town of Simrishamn (right). The adjacent region of Småland, though geographically less hospitable than Skåne, also offers some lovely towns, including Kalmar (center right) and Gränna (bottom right). Overleaf: magnificent twelfth-century Kalmar Castle.

Bohuslän, the region stretching north along the Swedish coast from Gothenburg, is famous for its lovely scenery. The area, which is characterized by pretty harbors like Kyrkesund Harbor (facing page), on Tjörn Island, has been a popular vacation destination for over a century. The nearby island of Marstrand (below) is dominated by seventeenth-century Carlsten Castle. Left: Dragmark Harbor, at Näset.

*Götaplatsen (below), an impressive square built in commemoration of Gothenburg's 300th anniversary, is the city's cultural heart, with the Museum of Fine Arts, Municipal Theater, Municipal Library and the City Concert Hall flanking its sides. Carl Milles' famous statue of Poseidon presides over the fountain in the square's center. Facing page top: stately buildings in Norra Hamngatan. Facing page bottom: Gustsav Adolfs Torg. Overleaf: the Maritime Museum, Gothenburg.*

33

Örebro Castle (below), a beautiful sixteenth-century Renaissance castle in the town of Örebro – the capital of the Swedish province of Närke – stands on an island in the Svartån. Neoclassical Rottneros Manor (facing page bottom), in the province of Värmland, is set in a beautiful park and boasts a superb collection of sculpture. Facing page top: the old stone bridge at Karlstad, capital of Värmland. Right: frozen Tännfors falls at Åre

*The city hall or Stadshuset (above), Stockholm, is situated on Kungsholmen, or King's Island. Riddarholmen, or the Isle of the Knights, can be seen through its colonnades. Stockholm Cathedral (above left), stands on Gamla Stan, in the center of the city. Left: Drottningholm Palace, on the island of Lovön. Below left: the Grand, Stockholm's best-known hotel. Facing page top: Sergels Torg. Facing page bottom: Riddarholmen and Stadshuset. Overleaf: the Old Town and Riddarholmen.*

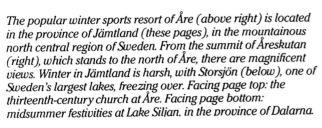

The popular winter sports resort of Åre (above right) is located in the province of Jämtland (these pages), in the mountainous north central region of Sweden. From the summit of Åreskutan (right), which stands to the north of Åre, there are magnificent views. Winter in Jämtland is harsh, with Storsjön (below), one of Sweden's largest lakes, freezing over. Facing page top: the thirteenth-century church at Åre. Facing page bottom: midsummer festivities at Lake Silian, in the province of Dalarna.

The Norwegian capital, Oslo, boasts some lovely buildings, among them the Royal Palace (left) and the Storting or parliament (below left). Near the Storting lies the Stortorget (below), the city's market square. Only a short distance from the city itself stands the famous Holmenkollen ski jump (above left). The most popular attraction of the town of Lillehammer is the Maihaugen Open-Air Museum (above). Facing page top: a panoramic view of Lillehammer. Facing page bottom: a view of Oslo by night. Overleaf: an aerial view of Oslo

The historic Norwegian city of Bergen (right and facing page bottom) was a base for the powerful Hanseatic League from the fourteenth to the sixteenth centuries, and reminders of the League, and the influence that it wielded, are found throughout the city. Bryggen (right), for example, on the northeastern side of Vågen – the city's harbor – was where the houses of the German merchants once stood. Stavanger (below) and Kristiansand (facing page top), like Bergen, are important ports situated on Norway's west coast.

From the top of Prekestolen (below), a sheer outcrop of rock reaching 1,960 feet in height, there are spectacular views of Lysefjord, near Stavanger. The scenery along Norway's west coast north of Stavanger, is renowned the world over for its beauty. Magnificent fjords framed by snow-capped mountains, like Nordfjord (bottom right), lovely waterfalls like that at Briksdal (center right), on Innvikfjord, and rugged mountain peaks like Romsdalshorn (right), give the area its unique character. Overleaf: Geiranger Fjord, often considered the most beautiful of Norway's fjords.

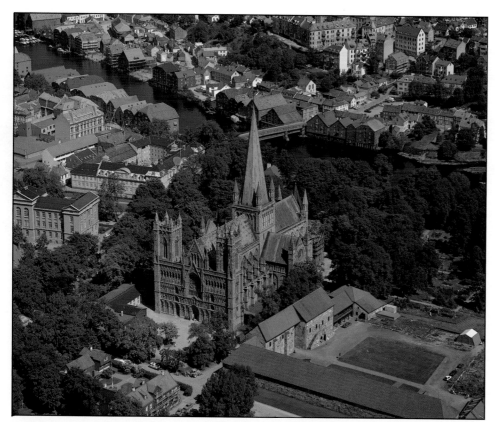

Trondheim (below), located on Trondheimfjord at the mouth of the River Nid, was Norway's first capital. The city is dominated by Nidaros Cathedral (left), one of Scandinavia's most beautiful churches. The cathedral – originally built in the eleventh century over the tomb of St. Olav, and later greatly enlarged – is evidence of the city's past wealth and importance. Facing page top: Kristiansund. Facing page bottom: Ålesund.

*Both Svolvær (above) and Henningsær (above right) are situated on Austvagøy, one of the Lofoten Islands. This string of rocky, mountainous islands off Norway's northwestern coast are renowned for charming, peaceful towns like Nusfjord (below right), on Flakstadøy, and Vaga Realsen (right). Like the spectacular Svartisen Glacier (below), on the Norwegian mainland, the islands lie within the Arctic Circle, in the Land of the Midnight Sun (overleaf). Facing page top: Torghatten. Facing page bottom: Reine, on the island of Moskenesøy.*

*The beauty of the glaciers in Magdalenefjord (left), on West Spitsbergen, is breathtaking, The island is the largest in the Spitsbergen archipelago – Norway's outpost in the Arctic Ocean – and it is here that Longyearbyen (below), the islands' largest city and administrative center, is located. Facing page top: Honningsvåg, on the southeastern coast of North Cape. Facing page bottom: Hammerfest, Europe's most northerly town. Overleaf: the lovely town of Tromsø. Following page: the midnight sun off the coast of North Cape.*

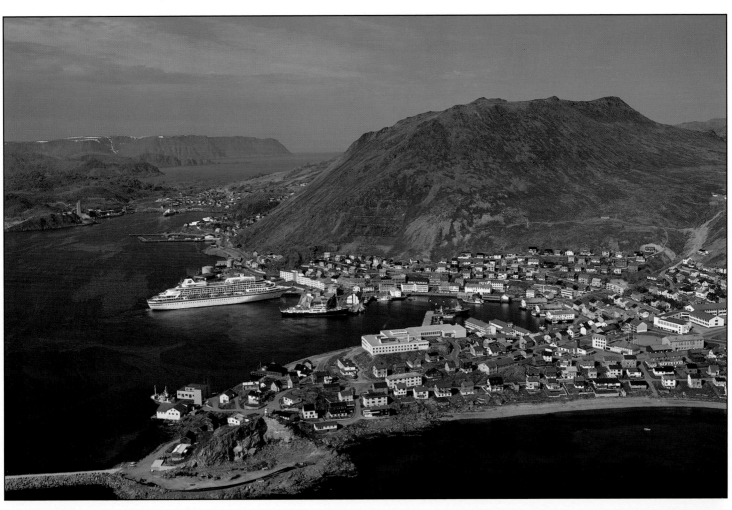